WAVES
OF INFLUENCE

Your Expanded Guide and Insight to Your Highest Self

Original text and photography by
Bernadette Johnson
(unless otherwise attributed)

To JD
Be the Wave!

Much Love
Bernadette Johnson

ISBN 978-1-5483-5205-9

DEDICATION
AND ACKNOWLEDGMENTS

This book is dedicated to my babies,
Damon Brown, Dr. Parul Patel Brown, Alec & Abhi

I must give acknowledgments to the many who have shared their most favorite, life-altering quotes with me in hopes they would inspire others. The compilation of the chosen quotes has been collected on napkins, backs of envelopes, via email/text, scraps of paper and post-its. Be inspired!

INTRODUCTION

Quotes have played an essential role throughout my life. Some quotes have had a way of getting me over an issue ... some quotes have acted as a point of enlightenment and then there were some so profound that they brought tears to my eyes.

I titled the original book *Waves of Influence* because that's how quotes have emerged in my life ... as waves washing over me mentally, physically and spiritually. A quote also allows us to bear witness ... to create a space ... for the author of the quote to share their deepest thinking, their burning question or their enlightened moment.

Waves of Influence is arranged by themes that reflect how our pursuits, our challenges and our joys emerge in our everyday lives. Each theme begins with a thought provoking insight, followed by the inspirational quotes. This gives the reader freedom to choose a theme that resonates with them or maybe to do a 'quote of the day'. Then each chapter ends with "Waves of Wonder". It's an opportunity to WOW ourselves by putting thoughts into action.

This expanded edition will enable you to explore each chapter more deeply…helping you to drill down to reveal your untapped wisdom. I am so excited you decided to accept the challenge and lean into your strengths!

My wish is for you to find solace, inspiration and insight from this body of work. Perhaps something that sparks your passion and pushes you out of your comfort zone or calls to your highest self.

I invite you to share your experience with the Waves of Influence community on Facebook: Influence the Wave.

Bernadette Johnson
East Lansing, MI

TABLE
OF CONTENTS

LET'S GET
UNCOMFORTABLE...

"The day came when the risk to remain tight in a bud was more painful than the risk it took to blossom." - Anais Nin

It takes courage to choose to be uncomfortable … to choose to be out of your comfort zone. It's a scary proposition because you are making a choice to be vulnerable ... to open yourself up to criticism, judgment and possibly ridicule. Ironically, most of this diatribe happens in our own minds. You know that little voice in your head, we'll call it a "gremlin", that tells you everything from "you can't do this" to "you're not smart enough" to "no one has ever done that".

We all have those voices in our head when we're about to step outside of our comfort zone. Your 'gremlin' may be saying something different to you ... but it's definitely not serving your highest self. My personal plan of action has become, for every reason my gremlin tells me I can't do something, I have a rebuttal for why I can.

Score so far:

Bernadette: Most of the time
Gremlin: On occasion ... temporarily

The choice to shift, as Anais Nin shares, is when the desire for what you want outweighs what you fear. I invite you to step outside of your comfort zone ... you're in good company!

A man and his son were walking in the forest. Suddenly the boy trips and feeling a sharp pain he screams, "Ahhhhh."

Surprised, he hears a voice coming from the mountain, "Ahhhhh!"

Filled with curiosity, he screams: "Who are you?", but the only answer he receives is: "Who are you?"

This makes him angry, so he screams: "You are a coward!", and the voice answers: "You are a coward!"

He looks at his father, asking, "Dad, what is going on?"

"Son," the man replies, "pay attention!" Then he screams, "I admire you!"

The voice answers: "I admire you!"

The father shouts, "You are wonderful!", and the voice answers: "You are wonderful!"

The boy is surprised, but still can't understand what is going on.

Then the father explains, "People call this 'ECHO', but truly it is 'LIFE!' Life always gives you back what you give out!

Life is a mirror of your actions. If you want more love, give more love! If you want more kindness, give more kindness! If you want understanding and respect, give understanding and respect! If you want people to be patient and respectful to you, give patience and respect! This rule of nature applies to every aspect of our lives."

Life always gives you back what you give out. Your life is not a coincidence, but a mirror of your own doings.

~Author Unknown

"Give me a lever long enough and a place to stand
and I can move the earth."
- Archimedes

"There are two mistakes one can make along the
road to truth ... not going all the way and not
starting."
- Buddha

"Fear is the cheapest room in the house. I would
like to see you living in better conditions."
- Hafiz

"If you accept a limiting belief, then it will become
a truth for you."
- Louise Hay

"The smallest action is always better than the
noblest of intentions."
- Robin Sharma

"I can be changed by what happens to me, but I
refuse to be reduced by it."
- Maya Angleou

"It's not what you are that holds you back; it's
what you think you're not."
- Denis Waitley

"Devote today to something so daring even you
can't believe you're doing it."
- Oprah Winfrey

"In every success story you find someone who has
made a courageous decision."
- Peter Drucker

"We all have big changes in our lives that are more
or less a second chance."
- Harrison Ford

"How does one become a butterfly? You must
want to fly so much that you are willing to give up
being a caterpillar."
- Trina Paulus

"You are the only problem you will ever have and you are the only solution."
- Jim Rohn

"Fearlessness is not being afraid of who you are."
- Chogyan Trungpa

"It's not the events of our lives that shape us, but our beliefs as to what those events mean."
- Tony Robbins

"Nothing is permanent, but change ... it is in changing that things find purpose."
- Heraclitus

"The difference between a stumbling block and a stepping stone is how you use them."
- Unknown

"Change will not come if we wait for some other person or some other time. We are the ones we've been waiting for. We are the change that we seek."
- President Barack Obama

WAVES OF WONDER

Insight Question:

When was the last time you did something for the first time? If you can't remember it's time to start. Begin with: I have always wanted to:

Deeper Dive Questions:

What draws you to this desire?

What story have you been telling yourself about why you cannot? Is it true?

Call to action:

What are you willing to embrace to make this happen?

What are you willing to release to make this happen?

NOTES

BETWEEN
A ROCK AND A HARD PLACE...

"When one door closes, another opens; but we often look so long and so regretfully upon the closed door that we do not see the one which has opened for us."
- Alexander Graham Bell

Life is such a treasured journey. We sometimes forget this when we get bogged down with the day to day ... particularly when we hit a patch of disappointments, a string of frustrations, being overwhelmed or just being in a funk. Although we're unhappy about where we are, it appears to be easier to stay in this place, but in reality we are stuck.

At this critical moment, we must ask ourselves how we are protected or benefited by staying where we are. Just think about it, if we were not, we would have moved on by now. It could be that if we stay in this place, we won't have to make a decision? It could be that we will not have to step out on our

own? It could be, by focusing on others, it gives us an excuse not to focus on ourselves? Or it could simply be that we're afraid to move forward? The bigger question is what is it costing us to stay in this state of mind? Precious time? Relationships? Happiness?

You see, we've forgotten that we have a choice in our thinking, which directly impacts our actions. In doing this we will discover that we have all we need ... we are enough ... just as we are ... we have enough to step into our greatness and use our energy to choose those things that serve our highest potential.

A Carrot, An Egg, And A Coffee Bean

A young woman went to her mother and told her about her life and how things were so hard for her. She did not know how she was going to make it and wanted to give up. She was tired of fighting and struggling. It seemed as if as soon as one problem was solved a new one arose.

Her mother took her to the kitchen. She filled three pots with water and placed each on a high fire. Soon the pots came to a boil. In the first, she placed carrots, in the second she placed eggs, and the last she placed ground coffee beans. She let them sit and boil, without saying a word.

In about twenty minutes she turned off the burners. She fished the carrots out and placed them in a bowl. She pulled the eggs out and placed them in a bowl. Then she ladled the coffee out and placed it in a bowl.

Turning to her daughter, she asked, "Tell me, what do you see?" "Carrots, eggs, and coffee," she replied.

She brought her closer and asked her to feel the carrots. She did and noted that they were soft. She then asked her to take an egg and break it. After pulling off the shell, she observed the hard-boiled egg. Finally, she asked her to sip the coffee. The daughter smiled, as she tasted its rich aroma. The daughter then asked. "What does it mean, mother?"

Her mother explained that each of these objects had faced the same adversity - boiling water - but each reacted differently. The carrot went in strong, hard, and unrelenting. However, after being subjected to the boiling water, it softened and became weak.

The egg had been fragile. Its thin outer shell had protected its liquid interior. But, after sitting through the boiling water, its inside became hard.

The ground coffee beans were unique, however. After they were in the boiling water, they had changed the water.

"Which are you?" she asked her daughter. "When adversity knocks on your door, how do you respond? Are you a carrot, an egg, or a coffee bean?"

The carrot seemed strong, but with pain and adversity, it wilted and became soft and lost its strength?

The egg that started with a malleable heart, but changed with the heat. It had a fluid spirit, but after a death, a breakup, a financial hardship or some other trial, it hardened and stiffened? Its shell still looks the same, but on the inside it became bitter and tough with a stiff spirit and hardened heart.

The coffee bean actually changed the hot water, the very circumstance that brought the pain. When the water got hot, the bean released the fragrance and flavor.

Are you like the bean? When things are at their worst, do you get better and change the situation around you?

When the hour is the darkest and trials are at their greatest, do you elevate to another level? How do you handle adversity? Are you a carrot, an egg, or a coffee bean?

-Author Unknown

"It's choice, not chance that determines your
destiny."
- Aristotle

"Crying doesn't indicate you're weak. Since birth,
it has always been a sign that you are, in fact,
alive."
- Unknown

"If you don't go after what you want, you'll never
have it. If you don't ask, the answer is always no.
If you don't step forward, you're always in the
same place."
- Nora Roberts

"Sometimes in the winds of change we find our
true direction."
- Unknown

"Not everything that is faced can be changed ... but
nothing can be changed until it is faced."
- James Baldwin

"An old belief is like an old shoe. We so value its
comfort that we fail to notice the hole in it."
- Robert Brault

"I keep the telephone of my mind open to peace, harmony, health, love and abundance. Then, whenever doubt, anxiety or fear, try to call me, they keep getting a busy signal ... and soon they'll forget my number."
- Edith Armstrong

"Worry never robs tomorrow of its sorrow, it only saps today of its joy."
- Leo Buscaglia

"If I had my life to live over, I would perhaps have more actual troubles but I'd have fewer imaginary ones."
- Don Herold

"Worry is like a rocking chair. It uses up all your energy, but where does it get you?"
- Bob Gass

"A thought which does not result in an action is nothing much ... and an action which does not proceed from a thought is nothing at all."
- Unknown

"The world has the habit of making room for the man whose words and actions show that he knows where he is going."
- Napoleon Hill

"What worries you, masters you."
- Haddon W. Robinson

"I would rather have a mind opened by wonder than one closed by belief."
- Gerry Spence

"With every day is a new challenge and with every new challenge is a new you."
- Mary Marshall

"Courage doesn't always roar. Sometimes it is the quiet voice at the end of the day saying ... I will try again tomorrow."
- Mary Anne Radmacher

"If we all did the things we are capable of doing, we would literally astound ourselves."
- Thomas A. Edison

WAVES OF WONDER

Insight Question:

What in your current life provides the seeds for the future you want to create?

Deeper Dive Questions:

Which "seed" most excites you?

Why?

Call to action:

What small, yet powerful step can you make to grow this "seed"?

What are you willing to commit to make this happen in the next week?

NOTES

I CAN SEE
CLEARLY NOW

"If you want the rainbow, you gotta put up with the rain."
- Dolly Parton

A wise person once shared with me, that contrast is not a bad thing. It is there for us to gain clarity for what we most want by exposing us to what we do not want.

It is hard to see this when we are in the midst of disruption. We often ask ourselves, why is this happening to me? We beat ourselves up ... blaming, cursing and reviewing all of our actions, searching for the culprit. The funny thing is...we all get a turn. Contrast is an equal opportunity employer. Think of this contrast, as your turn ... your turn to grow from this experience ... your turn to embrace this disparity ... your turn to fine tune what you truly desire.

We sometimes forget that life is cyclical. Everything has a season ... a rhythm that we actually flow with naturally ... if we allow. Some of us fight so hard to keep the status quo that we may miss those sweet and precious gifts that emerge just on

the other side of contrast. We must learn to forgive ourselves ... be gentle with our spirit.

So the next time you are in contrast ... stand tall ... look it straight in the eye ... and say "hello, dear friend ... what am I to learn from you today?"

The Cracked Pot

Everyday a farmer carried two pots to the river to fetch water. Each pot hung on the end of a pole across his shoulders. The pot on his right side was new and perfect. The pot on his left side was older and had a crack in its side.

The new pot brought back all the water the farmer put into it. But the cracked pot leaked out water in a little trail. This went on day after day for two years. The little cracked pot felt terrible. "I am so ashamed of my imperfection!" One day, it spoke to the farmer. "I must apologize. I only deliver half my load because leak out water all the way back to your house. You should just get rid of me!"

The farmer said, "Do not despair. Look behind you. Do you not see the beautiful flowers along the path? Those are on the left side where I carry you. I knew about your special feature so I planted flower seeds and you have watered those seeds as I walked hoe. Thanks to you, I have fresh flowers for my table. Thank you, little cracked pot. You are very special."

-Hindu Tale

"Difficulties arise in our lives, not to obstruct, but to instruct."
- Brian Tracy

"I never said it would be easy, I only said it would be worth it."
- Mae West

"There is no such thing as a problem without a gift for you in its hands."
- Richard Bach

"Life consists not in holding good cards, but in playing those you hold, well."
- Paul Martinelli

"Do not look where you fell, but where you slipped."
- African Proverb

"The fishermen know that the sea is dangerous and the storm terrible, but they have never found these dangers sufficient reasons for remaining ashore."
- Vincent Van Gogh

"No man ever steps into the same river twice ... for it is not the same river and he is not the same man."
- Heraclitus

"Try to do what's right versus what's easy ... it doesn't always have to be done perfect, stay positive ... it will get you through the tough times and remember to have fun along the way."
- Jim Costello

"Take the first step in faith. You don't have to see the whole staircase, just take the first step."
- Martin Luther King, Jr.

"The brick walls are there for a reason. The brick walls are not there to keep us out; the brick walls are there to give us a chance to show how badly we want something."
- Randy Pausch

"The pessimist sees difficulty in every opportunity. The optimist sees the opportunity in every difficulty."
- Winston Churchill

"If you don't like something, change it. If you can't change it, change your attitude."
- Maya Angelou

"In any moment of decision the best thing you can do is the right thing. The worst thing you can do is nothing."
- Theodore Roosevelt

"We can choose how we respond even when we do not get to choose what has happened."
- Paul Wesselman

"Nurture your mind with great thoughts for you will never go any higher than you think."
- Benjamin Disraeli

"Wisdom is knowing the right path to take, integrity is taking it."
- M.H McKee

"All personal breakthroughs begin with a change in beliefs."
- Anthony Robbins

WAVES OF WONDER

Insight Question:

What do you know today, that you didn't know yesterday, that will serve you tomorrow?

Deeper Dive Questions:

Why did this wisdom resonate with you?

What are some examples of how this piece of wisdom might serve you going forward?

Call to action:

What steps will you put in place to ensure you don't forget this wisdom you've gained?

NOTES

I GET BY
WITH A LITTLE HELP...

"Whatever life we have experienced, if we can tell our story to someone who listens, we find it easier to deal with our circumstances."
- Margaret J. Wheatley

Our lives are made up of stories ... sometimes it is one story at a time ... sometimes it's a group of stories happening simultaneously. What is most common is that our stories usually include other people ... who witness our lives. We call them by many names: our circle ... our tribe ... our friends ... our Peeps! Having the right people surrounding us can be a lighthouse when we feel lost, be a centering magnet when we're off kilter and a cheering squad when we need support. They are the ones, as the saying goes, who lift us to our feet when our wings have trouble remembering how to fly.

As we think about the people we have in our lives ... how do we know if we have the right people surrounding us? The best way to measure this, is by how we feel after an interaction with them. Do we feel supported? Do we feel heard? Do we sometimes laugh so hard that our side hurts ... only to start laughing again? Do we feel safe enough to cry ... from a whimper to full fledge bawling like a child?

The right people will allow us to be in a funk ... but only for enough time to feel it and then announce ... O.K ... that's enough. They don't judge us. They accept us for who we are ... warts and all. They want the best for us. They are just as excited about our new haircut as they are about the new job promotion. They are just as sad about throwing away our favorite pair old shoes as they are about the breakup with the love of our lives. You see ... these folks are those special people who share your joy as well as your pain. They bear witness to the magnificent and wondrous miracle that is our life.

STORY OF DAMON AND PYTHIAS

There lived in those days in Syracuse two young men called Damon and Pythias. They were very good friends, and loved each other so dearly that they were hardly ever seen apart.

Now it happened that Pythias in some way roused the anger of the tyrant, who put him in prison, and condemned him to die in a few days. When Damon heard of it, he was in despair, and vainly tried to obtain his friend's pardon and release.

The mother of Pythias was very old, and lived far away from Syracuse with her daughter. When the young man heard that he was to die, he was tormented by the thought of leaving the women alone. In an interview with his friend Damon, Pythias regretfully said that he would die easier had he only been able to bid his mother good-by and find a protector for his sister.

Damon, anxious to gratify his friend's last wish, went into the presence of the tyrant, and proposed to take the place of Pythias in prison, and even on the cross, if need be, provided the latter were allowed to visit his relatives once more.

Dionysius had heard of the young men's touching friendship, and hated them both merely because they were good; yet he allowed them to change places, warning them both however, that, if Pythias were not back in time, Damon would have to die in his stead.

At first Pythias refused to allow his friend to take his place in prison, but finally he consented, promising to be back in a few days to release him. So Pythias hastened home, found a husband for his sister, and saw her safely married. Then after providing for his mother and bidding her farewell, he set out to return to Syracuse.

The young man was traveling alone and on foot. He soon fell into the hands of thieves, who bound him fast to a tree; and it was only after hours of desperate struggling that he managed to wrench himself free once more, and sped along his way.

He was running as hard as he could to make up for lost time, when he came to the edge of a stream. He had crossed it easily a few days before; but a sudden spring freshet had changed it into a raging torrent, which no one else would have ventured to enter.

In spite of the danger, Pythias plunged into the water, and, nerved by the fear that his friend would die in his stead, he fought the waves so successfully that he reached the other side safe but almost exhausted.

Regardless of his pains, Pythias pressed anxiously onward, although his road now lay across a plain, where the hot rays of the sun and the burning sands greatly increased his fatigue and faintness, and almost made him die of thirst. Still he sped onward as fast as his trembling limbs could carry him; for the sun was sinking fast, and he knew that his friend would die if he were not in Syracuse by sunset.

Dionysius, in the meanwhile, had been amusing himself by taunting Damon, constantly telling him that he was a fool to have risked his life for a friend, however dear.

To anger him, he also insisted that Pythias was only too glad to escape death, and would be very careful not to return in time.

Damon, who knew the goodness and affection of his friend, received these remarks with the scorn they deserved, and repeated again and again that he knew Pythias would never break his word, but would be back in time, unless hindered in some unforeseen way.

The last hour came. The guards led Damon to the place of crucifixion, where he again asserted his faith in his friend, adding, however, that he sincerely hoped Pythias would come too late, so that he might die in his stead.

Just as the guards were about to nail Damon to the cross, Pythias dashed up, pale, bloodstained, and disheveled, and flung his arms around his friend's neck with a sob of relief. For the first time, Damon now turned pale, and began to shed tears of bitter regret.

In a few hurried, panting words, Pythias explained the cause of his delay, and, loosening his friend's bonds with his own hands, bade the guards bind him instead.

Dionysius, who had come to see the execution, was so touched by this true friendship, that for once he forgot his cruelty, and let both young men go free, saying that he would not have believed such devotion possible had he not seen it with his own eyes.

-Greek Legend

"Friends give us the courage to lift the blinds on our hearts, to open up and show what we generally keep hidden from the rest of the world."
- Unknown

"When spider webs unite, they can halt even a lion."
- African Proverb

"No road is long with good company."
- Turkish Proverb

"Relationships are all there is. Everything in the universe only exists because it is in relationship to everything else. Nothing exists in isolation. We have to stop pretending we are individuals that can go it alone."
- Margaret Wheatley

"Everyone needs a place to hear their heart speak."
- Valerie Young

"To go faster, go alone. To go further, go together."
- African Proverb

"As we let our own light shine, we unconsciously give other people permission to do the same. "
- Marianne Williamson

"You get the best out of people not by lighting a fire beneath them, but by lighting a fire within them."
- Bob Nelson

"Believing in people before they have proved themselves is the key to motivating people to reach their potential. "
- John Maxwell

"It's always worthwhile to make others aware of their worth."
- Malcolm Forbes

"In everyone's life, at some time, our inner fire goes out. It is then burst into flame by an encounter with another human being. We should all be thankful for those people who rekindle the inner spirit."
- Albert Schweitzer

"They may forget what you said, but they will never forget how you made them feel."
- Carl W. Buechner

"As you move through your day, make choices so that when you close your eyes at the end of the day, you will be able to say ... This was a day worth living."
- David Simon

"Service to others is the rent you pay for your room here on earth."
- Muhammad Ali

"Love and compassion are not luxuries, they are necessities."
- Dali Llama

"When we seek to discover the best in others, we somehow bring out the best in ourselves."
- William Arthur

"We are together, I forget the rest."
- Walt Whitman

"There's nothing of significance that you can do by yourself."
- Eckart Tolle

WAVES OF WONDER

Insight Question:

What five people can help you to change the world?

Deeper Dive Questions:

What traits draws you to these people?

Call to action:

How will you deepen your relationship with them?

How will you share your passions/quests with them?

NOTES

FINDING
PURPOSE

There are two great days in a person's life: the day they are born and the day they discover why.

- John Maxwell

Have you thought about your 'why'... your purpose? Most of us have asked ourselves this question over the years. Discovering our purpose is such a powerful journey. Our purpose gives us our reason for being here ... on this earth ... at this time ... in this place. Our purpose should be so large that it directs our choices, manifests our desires, and creates a drive for the accomplishment of the perceived impossible ... it's that great.

Often as we begin to seek our purpose, we encounter paralysis of analysis. That is, we've clouded our thoughts with the dreaded 'how' of it all before our purpose is even fully developed. We start down the path of feeling good about it and then begin to pick it apart at the seams with ... how will I find the time ... how will I get the money to do this ... how will I get support ... how am I going to get it done?

The beauty of a purpose that is nurtured and allowed to develop is that it inspires your heart. It attaches itself to your very core. When you think about your purpose ... your breath actually catches ... your heart beats a little faster ... you have a smile that radiates from within. From this perspective the "how" doesn't matter, because you understand the reason you ARE!

The Carpenter's House

An elderly carpenter was ready to retire. He told his employer-contractor of his plans to leave the house-building business and live a more leisurely life with his wife enjoying his extended family.

He would miss the paycheck, but he needed to retire. They could get by. The contractor was sorry to see his good worker go and asked if he could build just one more house as a personal favor. The carpenter said yes, but in time it was easy to see that his heart was not in his work. He resorted to shoddy workmanship and used inferior materials.

It was an unfortunate way to end his career.

When the carpenter finished his work and the builder came to inspect the house, the contractor handed the front-door key to the carpenter. "This is your house," he said, "my gift to you."

What a shock! What a shame! If he had only known he was building his own house, he would have done it all so differently. Now he had to live in the home he had built none too well.

So it is with us. We build our lives in a distracted way, reacting rather than acting, willing to put up less than the best. At important points we do not give the job our best effort. Then with a shock we look at the situation we have created and find that we are now living in the house we have built. If we had realized that, we would have done it differently.

Think of yourself as the carpenter. Think about your house. Each day you hammer a nail, place a board, or erect a wall. Build wisely. It is the only life you will ever build. Even if you live it for only one day more, that day deserves to be lived graciously and with dignity.

The plaque on the wall says, "Life is a do-it-yourself project." Your life tomorrow will be the result of your attitudes and the choices you make today.

~ Unknown Author

"Opportunity dances with those already on the dance floor."
- H. Jackson Brown Jr.

"And those who were seen dancing were thought to be insane by those who could not hear the music."
- Nietzsche

"Everyone has been made for some particular work and the desire for that work has been put in every heart."
- Rumi

"Chance favors the prepared mind."
- Benjamin Franklin

"A great life is born in the soul, grown in the mind and lived from the heart."
- Suzanne Zoglio

"Too many of us are not living our dreams because we are living our fears."
- Les Brown

"Your why should make you cry."
- Ken Dunn

"If your 'why' is big enough, the 'how' doesn't matter."
- Unknown

"Don't ask yourself what the world needs; ask yourself what makes you come alive. And then go and do that. Because what the world needs is people who have come alive."
- Howard Thurman

"Before the beginning of great brilliance, there must be chaos. Before a brilliant person begins something great, they must look foolish in the crowd."
- I Ching

"There is no passion to be found playing small – in settling for a life that is less than the one you are capable of living."
- Nelson Mandela

"Unless you do something beyond what you have already mastered, you will never grow."
- Ralph Waldo Emerson

"Life isn't about finding yourself. Life is about creating yourself."
- George Bernard Shaw

"Far away there in the sunshine are my highest aspirations. I may not reach them, but I can look up and see their beauty, believe in them and try to follow where they lead."
- Louisa May Alcott

"The greatest danger for most of us is not that our goal is too high and we miss it, but too low and we achieve it."
- Michelangelo

"It's better to have something to remember than anything to regret".
- Frank Zappa

"Nothing limits achievement like small thinking; nothing expands possibilities like unleashed imagination."
- William Arthur Ward

WAVES OF WONDER

Insight Question:

What gifts do you bring to the world?

What gifts do you seek from the world?

Deeper Dive Questions:

What were the times that your gifts served you well and how?

How would your life be different if you did more of what you really loved to do?

Call to action:

If what we focus on becomes our reality, how will you shift your thinking to use your gifts?

What is a potential upcoming opportunity where your gifts will serve you well?

NOTES

APPRECIATION

I offer my sincere appreciation to my son, author, Damon Brown for his fierce support, his generosity of guidance and unconditional love that he's always given. Thank you for believing in my dream of writing Waves of Influence enough to publish and launch the electronic version and editing both print versions.

My deepest gratitude to one of the most creative people I know, Julie Becker. Thank you so much for designing the print copy of Waves of Influence and designing the cover for this Expanded Edition. You have always exhibited such passion, creativity and diligence for all the important details that make a book inviting!

I also want to share my appreciation to my sister-friends (Yvonne, Julia, Hilda, Ann, Anne, Jodi, Robin, Fonda, Vicky and Jackie) who have always been, not just my biggest cheerleaders, but the staunchest advocates for my highest self.

Lastly, I offer appreciation to my family, who always believed I can do anything!

ABOUT
THE AUTHOR

Bernadette Johnson

Greetings!

As a Leadership Consultant and Collaboration Strategist, I help businesses leverage their return on leadership. I am dedicated to creating fertile ground for developing greatness in established and emerging leaders by building environments that nurture the human spirit while simultaneously achieving business results. When we partner, we will achieve breakthrough results by transforming the way your leaders lead and how they learn!

I will be your greatest ally for:
- Leadership Development
- Team Cohesion
- Strategic Guidance for Leaders
- Collaboration Strategies
- Transition Management

I invite you to learn more at my website: http://BernadetteJohnson.com. Some of my offerings include: leadership development, keynotes, strategic guidance sessions, workshops and leadership retreats. Want to receive monthly leadership wisdom? Join other amazing leaders at http://bernadettejohnson.com/blog!

Much grace,
Bernadette

80079336R00049

Made in the USA
Columbia, SC
03 November 2017